Love Yourself First

7 STEPS TO FINDING & HEALING THE REAL YOU

CAROLYN MONDEN

This publication is designed to educate and provide general information regarding the subject matter based on the author's experiences. It is published with the understanding that neither the author nor the publisher is engaged in rendering professional counseling services. They are not intended to be a definitive set of instructions for your personal situation. The information is presented as is and the author nor the publisher make no representations or warranties of any kind with respect to the book's contents. Always consult your doctor or mental health professional for your individual needs.

For more information about the author's life coaching and healing work, go to www.carolynmonden.com.

DEDICATION

For my beloved aunt Jackie,
you are my inspiration in life and beyond.

To Benny and Charlotte,
I hope to lead by example. Follow your dreams.

"Loving yourself is the greatest revolution."
—Rima Mullins

Table of Contents

Love Yourself First

7 STEPS TO FINDING & HEALING THE REAL YOU

By

CAROLYN MONDEN

SUNFLOWER
PUBLISHING

Introduction

The most important relationship you'll ever have is the one with yourself. Yet, it's the hardest relationship to start and it's the one we repeatedly neglect. As an intuitive life coach, my work is centered on helping clients learn to love themselves. I use my natural psychic gifts to uncover behavior patterns and life paths to assist my clients on their journey to be their best selves. How we see ourselves sets the tone for how we view the world. If you are unable to accept yourself on any level, it will be challenging to do the difficult work of loving yourself.

For many years, I ran a race I wasn't aware I'd entered. Life was happening and I wasn't (properly) prepared to live it. Our society is set up for non-stop participation, with social media distractions and over-committed schedules. There's zero time for loving and healing ourselves and because of this we've conflated achievement and doing with fulfillment and love. None of this provides the love we desperately need.

Ten years into my relationship with my husband is when I finally understood how much he loved me. Can you believe that it took a decade? Before we met, I'd spent my life wanting someone to rescue me and in some ways, my husband did that, but his love wasn't enough to fill the void. To become whole is an inside job, so it was my job to find out what was missing and see myself through a loving lens. I attacked this task the way a scientist goes about curing a disease. I dug deep to pull up the root of my issues and I shined a light on my ugly, unpleasant repressed pain and emotions. This led me to discover parts of myself I'd stored away for protection. This wasn't an easy process, but I was determined to do this to become whole. During this journey, I became my own teacher, healer, sister, mother and friend.

Wholeness of the self means accepting and healing every bit of the shameful, rejected parts that shunned by the world around me. I had to meet myself in places I once deemed unworthy of love. I had to learn to stop feeding the monster within and refuse to allow it to color my world.

And now it's your turn. This may sound scary and hard, because it is, and it takes being committed to yourself, which brings me to how you should use this book. I created seven steps to help start the healing process and begin self-acceptance, even if you do it in small doses. Each chapter contains my struggle story and how I used the steps to get to where I am today. In each chapter, there are affirmations, exercises and journal entries. Please follow the steps and complete the exercises in order because each one prepares you for the next. *Love Yourself First* is not about repeating affirmations. An affirmation without action is just a wish. This book is meant to empower you and set you on the path to improved awareness.

My hope is with the help of this book, you recognize how amazing you are, how much is already perfect within you. How much the world needs you and your gift. I hope these steps activate a new journey, one filled with self-discovery, mindfulness, joy, meaning and love. I've walked these seven steps and it has allowed me to have the life of my dreams. While there is nothing wrong with having a house, car, or a profitable business, those items weren't part of my dream. The life of my dreams is about peace, gratitude, worthiness and the understanding that I matter. Each day, I'm in awe of all that has been waiting for me. I refuse to give up on myself and I refuse to let myself down. I know how to hold myself accountable and make magic for my well-being.

None of this would be possible if I didn't learn to love myself.

Step 1:

Be Honest With Yourself

AFFIRMATION:
I am honest about my story.

grew up in Washington Heights, yes, the same Latino neighborhood Lin-Manuel Miranda wrote a play about 15 years ago. It was one of the poorest neighborhoods in New York City in the 1980s and 1990s. Today, like many places in NYC (and around the country) gentrification has changed the look, feel and income bracket of my old stomping grounds. Back then, the odds were stacked against me. (Or so I thought.) My mother was a single mom and my brother and I lived with my grandparents in a violent home with little to no emotional support. We attended crowded, underserved public schools. My family made just enough to keep our heads above water. They did their best to provide for us, but basics like clothes, school supplies and our own beds weren't guaranteed. Love was provided in spurts.

As a kid, it was difficult for me to feel safe when my family and everyone in my neighborhood concentrated on day-to-day survival. My family did what they could, but I started to feel insecure. Maybe I knew too much too soon, including the fact that I was the result of an unplanned pregnancy. I believed my life was a mistake. No matter what I did, I never felt like I was enough, which fueled my thoughts of being unworthy. These elements became the breeding ground for my victim story.

Subconsciously, I self-sabotaged everything in my life to confirm my worst thoughts about myself. I was a smart kid and I knew my potential, but I often skipped school. As a teenager, escaping into books or movies was my way of dealing with not having enough space and not feeling loved which led me to fail high school. By the time, I decided to take control and focus on my studies, it was too late. I teetered between the desire to accomplish something to prove my worthiness while sabotaging opportunities to confirm my lack of love. These competing behaviors caused chaos and would follow me into adulthood. I had no idea that my internal unrest would influence every relationship, every interaction and every decision in my life. All that was broken within me would be made whole when I made the decision to be honest with myself.

Here's a simple, yet powerful thought. Change happens when we're ready to accept the truth, even if it's ugly. That means we have to sit with ourselves and unpack the tiny messes we've created and hidden in the dark and bring them to the light. That means we have to be willing to see things differently. That means we have to be willing to accept a new perception of ourselves.

Healing happens when we see the truth and leave behind what we've outgrown. Who you are is always changing, either you're willingly participating or you're resisting it. Who you desire to be is on the other side of the story you tell yourself. The good news is, and I'm proof of this, that your story can be re-written, but in order to do that, you have to take responsibility for how you've kept yourself in the dark.

CONSIDER THE FOLLOWING QUESTIONS:

1. Who are you when no one is looking?
2. Who do you want to be deep down in your soul?
3. What parts of yourself do you avoid because you're scared?
4. Who is the villain in your story? Your husband? Mom? Dad? Boss? Industry?
5. What stories do you tell yourself about why you're stuck?
6. Where do your tiny messes reside?
7. Where do you avoid taking responsibility?
8. What is your true story?

I decided to distance myself from my childhood story and create a life others would deem worthy. At 23 years old, I got married and moved to a respected neighborhood in Georgia to start a family. Soon, I started my dream job in public services and began manifesting my enoughness. Although I had everything I wanted, something wasn't right. While I searched for significance, I sunk deeper into the darkness of my story. Part of me didn't believe that I deserved this new life.

I never dealt with the pain of my story and I thought putting a mask on it or replacing it was the solution. The problem was the mask couldn't soothe the pain or teach me lessons about the past. All it did was push me further away from being fulfilled and my unworthiness chased me in my personal and professional life. During the first few years of my marriage, I'd pack up and leave my husband at the first sign of a disagreement. My faulty thought system was wired to break out if I thought he'd abandon me. The same behavior played out at work. I bounced around from good job to good job after a misunderstanding with co-workers or if my employer expressed disappointment. I dreaded being deserted, so I kept everyone at arm's length while requiring them to see and approve of me. I was desperate to belong but super afraid that no one would want me in his or her circle.

I couldn't enjoy my blessings because I didn't honor the girl who needed security. I needed to mourn with her and understand that it was okay to be the poor girl from the hood who dreamed about love, education and family who strived for more. Does this sound familiar?

Being stuck in my story kept me small. It kept me from moving forward. Foolishly, I thought that if people knew that I didn't have much, they would believe that I wasn't enough. My goal was to run away from that scared girl who didn't feel loved, but it didn't matter where I lived, my physical location meant nothing because I had to honor my truth. I could've chosen the easy route and blamed my parents and continued to live a life of victimhood, but I challenged myself to take responsibility for how I wanted to feel. We all have a story, but sometimes that story is not who you are. It doesn't have to define your life. Before deciding to write a new story, my career and marriage were merely Band-Aids on my wounds, until I became strong enough to face the parts of my childhood and young adulthood that caused me so much pain. As I started my healing journey, it became clear that I couldn't look to others to fix my life. I had to rebuild it piece by piece. I took responsibility for where and when I didn't show up for myself. I taught myself how to be honest. My childhood was a mess. Although I didn't have a strong foundation, it was my responsibility to take charge of my future, instead of offering excuses, instead of complaining and lamenting. It was time to do the work and I found my true self, piece by piece. I choose to be honest with myself. I put it all out on the table and even though my challenges were painful to acknowledge, I was able to see myself clearly. I was able to create a work in progress.

Here's your affirmation for this part of your journey: I am honest with myself.

Exercise 1: Write down your victim story.

_____

_____

_____

_____

_____

_____

_____

_____

Now that you've identified your story, you've taken the first step toward confronting it and making peace with it. Make this affirmation part of your new self-love practice. Say this, "I am not this story. I am enough." Every time you find yourself living in a false place in your mind, repeat those words. This affirmation will create a beautiful disruption that makes space for healing and brings you one step closer to loving yourself.

Exercise 2: Let's dig deeper into your victim story. Answer the following questions.

How does this story keep you small?

_____

_____

_____

_____

_____

_____

_____

_____

_____

_____

_____

_____

_____

_____

_____

_____

Why do you continue to identify with this story?

_____

_____

_____

_____

_____

_____

_____

_____

_____

_____

_____

_____

_____

_____

What do you need to move beyond this point in your life?

_____

_____

_____

_____

_____

_____

_____

_____

_____

_____

_____

_____

_____

_____

_____

_____

I learned about mirror work from Louise Hay. She's considered one of the founders of the self-help movement. Hay says mirror work is a chance to "connect with the inner child who has been neglected." In the next exercise, you are going to follow Hay's lead and hold a mirror up to your face and look at yourself. Then, you'll push yourself to look past what you normally see. Most of us look in the mirror and focus on the surface. Does my hair look okay? Are my eyebrows too fuzzy? Should I wax the hairs on my chin? Do I need to put on makeup?

Some women will glance at their reflection and say, "Oh, my nose is too big." Or "my face looks fat," if they decide to look at all. This is not about identifying your flaws. Some women aren't ready to look at themselves and be vulnerable with their internal spirit. Instead of tearing yourself down, build yourself up. This next exercise challenges you to celebrate yourself. It's okay to cry, especially if being kind and loving to yourself is unfamiliar territory. Don't beat yourself up if you cannot think of anything positive to say at the moment. Take a break and come back to it later. But make a commitment to try this exercise.

Exercise 3: Grab a small mirror or even a makeup compact and go into a quiet room or space. Take a good look at yourself without thinking about any external flaws. What do you see? Now, give yourself a compliment. Tell the woman in the mirror what you love about her.

How did the exercise make you feel?

_____

_____

_____

_____

_____

_____

_____

_____

_____

_____

_____

_____

IT'S TIME TO JOURNAL.

This is how I feel about being honest with myself.

_____

_____

_____

_____

_____

_____

_____

_____

_____

_____

_____

_____

_____

Carolyn Monden

Carolyn Monden

"

Healing happens
when we see the
truth and leave
behind what
we've outgrown.

"

Step 2:

Be Willing to Change

AFFIRMATION:
I am ready to heal.

The hardest part of releasing my story was refusing to see myself and my life from a fresh perspective. This meant giving up control of how and what needed to change because I was devoted to creating (and protecting) the new shiny exterior. To me, it didn't matter that I didn't know myself, even though I felt out of control in almost every setting and I relived old conversations and past scenarios. It was an oppressive cycle.

On top of that, I needed my husband, kids, co-workers and friends to accept me. To understand me in ways I didn't and couldn't understand myself. How could they do this when I didn't love, understand or accept myself? Secretly, I'd convinced myself that my life would make sense and have meaning if I followed a checklist and completed everything on it.

CAROLYN'S GOOD-LIFE CHECKLIST:

1. Great education
2. Loving marriage
3. Challenging career
4. Adoring family
5. Exciting social life

I'm happy to report that by age 33, I'd checked everything off the list and more blessings were headed my way. But you know what? I still wasn't happy. However, I'd convinced myself that all I needed to do was tweak the areas of my life that weren't running smoothly. In the fall of 2014, after my daughter's first birthday, I had an unsettling feeling as I stared at pictures of me and my beautiful little girl. I didn't recognize the woman in the photos. I couldn't identify with the woman holding my daughter or embracing my son and husband. It felt like I was looking at someone else's life.

Those pictures motivated me to make a change. Convinced that the 40 pounds I'd gained during my pregnancy were the real issue, I signed up for a 10-day juice detox that evening. I thought, "I will feel good about myself once I lose the weight." This is a control mindset. And if it didn't work, it wasn't my fault because "I am in control" of this. It was easier to blame someone else.

A few months rolled by before I started the detox. And I continued to question everyone else's behavior except mine. If I wasn't happy with my marriage, it was my husband's fault. If work wasn't fulfilling, management didn't know how to support me and my talents. If I hated my house, a new one would be better. I struggled to change everyone and everything around me, instead of taking a look in the mirror. In the previous chapter you read about my victim story, well, this one turned out to be my resistance story.

I finally started the detox on December 26, 2014. The first three days of the fast were the hardest. My body and mind were unable to handle the disruption to my system. But I focused on the goal because all of this torture would be worth it once I dropped 20 pounds. Day four was a little bit easier as my mind-body connection adjusted to the new arrangement. Still weak, I pushed through. Day five delivered a miracle. All of the loud noise in my head, all of the worry about the future and all of the recurring thoughts about the past had stopped. I was fully present and still for the first time in my life. My mind was clear. I saw past the stories (read: lies) I'd been telling myself. I saw my soul. I was at peace. And even though this feeling only lasted for a few seconds, it was enough to make me want more. From that day forward, I craved it. It was time to heal.

I quit my job three months after the detox. I struggled to fit in where I didn't belong and that workplace push and pull made me miserable. Resisting didn't work anymore. I surrendered. And in the process I began to make more changes and slowly, I started to find and accept the real me.

When we are unable to be with ourselves in the present moment, we cannot fully respond to life's questions. The more I resisted seeing my life as it really was in the moment, the more I suffered. I'm sure you've experienced this too. If you are like me, you've gotten stuck in a holding pattern and ended up reliving past mistakes. You didn't trust yourself and that lack of trust became part of your resistance. Nothing in my life was in alignment, but I misjudged redirections that came with the natural progression of life. My soul cried out for change, but I was in denial.

Here's your affirmation for this part of your journey: I am ready to see things differently.

Exercise 1: Be willing to see where you may be part of the problem.

Sometimes we blame others and avoid situations so that we don't have to change our way of thinking. We are too attached to outcomes. I was so devoted to my "good-life checklist" and consumed by how things looked to the outside world and what people thought, that I wasn't aware that my life was out of whack. Keeping up appearances was stressful and I didn't realize that I was missing out on life. It's difficult to release what doesn't serve us because we're used to it, it's familiar. We've grown comfortable with the suffering in our relationships, careers and friendships.

Carolyn Monden

What are you resisting that needs to change?

_____

_____

_____

_____

_____

_____

_____

_____

_____

_____

_____

_____

_____

_____

Why do you need this story to be true?

_____

_____

_____

_____

_____

_____

_____

_____

_____

_____

_____

_____

_____

_____

Exercise 2: List the things you are willing to change.

Example: I'm willing to commit to healing by having a difficult conversation with a toxic friend.

1.

  _____

  _____

2.

  _____

  _____

3.

  _____

  _____

4.

  _____

  _____

5.

  _____

  _____

Exercise 3: Practice mindfulness

According to the dictionary, mindfulness is a mental state that's achieved by focusing on the present moment, while calmly acknowledging and accepting your feelings, thoughts and bodily sensations. By practicing this therapeutic technique, we become keenly aware of what needs to change or when it's time to move away from people and situations that fail to nourish our well-being.

Step 1: Pay attention to your thoughts. Notice when you're stuck in the past, worried about the future or concerned about what people think. When you notice this happening, put the brakes on those thoughts and bring yourself back to the present moment.

Step 2: Remind yourself about the goodness that's currently happening. Are you at a wedding? Graduation? Cocktail party? Enjoy the conversation, the venue, the friends seated beside you. We cannot control the future and there's nothing we can do about the past. All we have is now.

Step 3: Find something to focus on. During my commute to work or even before bedtime, I noticed old repetitive thought patterns trying to creep in and wreak havoc on my life. My solution was to listen to audiobooks and guided meditations. This forced my mind to stay in the present and prevented me from slipping into my victim story.

Exercise 4: Start meditating

In order to see things clearly (and without resistance), a stillness practice is necessary. If you can stand to be still for 5-10 minutes a day, then you'll create the space to see what needs to change in your life. Don't be intimidated by meditation. Just focus on being quiet, being still and being in the moment. That means you cannot pick up the phone to call or text a friend. You cannot watch TV or check email. There aren't any brownie points for mediating and multitasking, so don't do it. The two don't belong together. Take this time to find a quiet place, close the door and be fully present in the moment.

HERE ARE A FEW WAYS TO DO THAT:

- Focus on your breath
- Scan your body for aches and pains or any sensation
- Be still, then journal for five minutes
- Go for a relaxing walk
- Just breathe

IT'S TIME TO JOURNAL.

This is how I feel about trading old beliefs
for something new.

_____

_____

_____

_____

_____

_____

_____

_____

_____

_____

_____

_____

_____

_____

Carolyn Monden

_____

_____

_____

_____

_____

_____

_____

_____

_____

_____

_____

_____

_____

_____

_____

_____

_____

Carolyn Monden

"

Sometimes
we blame others and
avoid situations so that
we don't have to change
our way of thinking.
We are too attached to
outcomes.

"

Step 3:

Face Your Fear

AFFIRMATION:
My will is strong.

Most people don't realize this but we live on autopilot. We're not intentional about how we move throughout our day or our lives. We're drifting through life without taking time to acknowledge hurt, disappointment or suffering because we're always steering clear of it. We live with persistent anxiety because the underlying fear hasn't been addressed. Believe it or not, anxiety is a manifestation of fear and it comes in all forms and being afraid occupies a large chunk of mental space.

Think about this, we're programmed to be in survival mode. We're wired to survive hunger and physical danger. It's part of our DNA. It's how we survive as a species and fear, in some cases, serves a purpose. In western society, the majority of needs are met. We no longer hunt and gather food. We can eat anytime we want and have it delivered to our doorstep. We're not in danger of animal attacks because we have shelter and tools to fend them off and wildlife encounters are rare as they stay away from populated areas. Our original human fears have manifested into psychological fears. Now, our mind needs to control our well-being and it creates fear where there isn't any.

Don't get me wrong, some of our fears are valid. It helps us avoid dangerous things like walking into oncoming traffic. But the unchecked emotion creates harmful life patterns. For instance, fear of abandonment is real for the woman that grew up without a father. Fear of homelessness is real if you lived in a shelter as a teen. However, as we get older and these fears, that are meant to "protect" us from harm, hurt us more than we know. The woman with abandonment issues never lets anyone get too close, and as a result, she never experiences real love or true commitment. Her fear keeps everyone at a distance as a form of protection. The person who is concerned about money may never pay attention to his or her finances for fear of seeing that buying that luxury car isn't in the budget. Or he or she may ignore their dwindling savings because money is being tossed out of the window. In both cases, this creates an unhealthy reactive life that reinforces our worst experiences. Unchecked fears become a permanent part of our personality.

Most adults are unaware of their fears because we have been programmed to shove them away. But in doing so we operate as fragmented parts of ourselves. You cannot love just one piece of yourself. You must love all of you, including your dark scary parts and your fears. Facing your fears builds emotional awareness that expands compassion for yourself and others.

No one wants to admit that she's controlled by her fears, but acknowledging and confronting it is the only way to finally be free. Some of my childhood memories were too painful to face, especially the feeling of being unloved or wanted. I wondered what people would think if they knew my parents didn't want me. My father had an affair with my mother and his family doesn't know I exist. My mother didn't want to tell my grandmother that she was pregnant (again) by a man she barely knew. I felt the pain of this secret relationship throughout my childhood. I felt like a burden. I didn't want to create trouble for my mother or grandmother so I made myself small.

As a child, I created this invisible world for myself and as an adult, I ran from and ended relationships because the vulnerability of needing someone and having them leave or half love me tapped into my deepest fear. By the time I decided it was time to heal and stop living from a place of fear, I'd forgotten most of my dark-corner memories. But that major fear? The fear that I wasn't enough was a hard and long process to fix. I cried. I had to ask that little girl to forgive me for rejecting her. We, my inner child and I, are still getting to know each other. I used the exercise below to get us started.

Here's your affirmation for this part of your journey: I can heal myself by getting to know my fears.

Exercise 1: See yourself as a child

Getting in touch with your inner child will help you begin to get comfortable with yourself. A good portion of our fears begin in childhood and when we go to the source, we start to understand where the fear started. This allows room for healing and feeling safe in our skin. Understanding the fear means it no longer has a hold over you or your behavior in certain situations.

Find a comfortable spot and close your eyes. Take a couple of breaths in through your nose and out through your mouth. Now, with your eyes still closed, picture yourself as a child. Talk to your younger self. Connect with that little person who was full of hope, love and excitement, but had it taken away. When you're done, answer the questions below.

How old are you? What are you wearing? Where are you?

_____

_____

_____

_____

_____

_____

_____

_____

_____

_____

_____

_____

_____

_____

_____

_____

Carolyn Monden

How do you feel when you look at your younger self?

_____

_____

_____

_____

_____

_____

_____

_____

_____

_____

_____

_____

_____

_____

Now, it's time to find out what your inner child needs. This may be odd at first. Try it a couple of times until you're comfortable with the exercise. Who you were as a child is who you are, this is the real you before fear robbed you of the peace that you're seeking as an adult. If you watch a two, three, even four-year-old child, you'll see how that kid reacts to life with joy and ease. Children possess a natural curiosity about life before parents and relatives introduce fear, trauma and pain. Babies do not fear anything when they're born. Fear is passed down from generation to generation and often, it isn't done with the intent to harm. Our families are merely teaching us survival techniques. It is time to understand and release them.

Carolyn Monden

Now ask your younger self, what do you need from me today?

_____

_____

_____

_____

_____

_____

_____

_____

_____

_____

_____

_____

_____

_____

_____

Exercise 2: Do the thing that makes you scared.

There is no better way to face your fear than to sit with it. One of my favorite ways to face a fear is to do something I've always wanted to do, but haven't because I feared failing, getting started or doing it alone. So now it's your turn.

List three things you've always wanted to do:

1.

_____

_____

2.

_____

_____

3.

_____

_____

Now, create a plan to complete one or all the things on the list! Commit to you. Remember, empowerment is not something you receive, rather it's created with your actions.

_____

_____

_____

_____

_____

_____

_____

_____

_____

_____

_____

_____

_____

_____

_____

IT'S TIME TO JOURNAL.

This is how I feel about slaying the fear dragon.

_____

_____

_____

_____

_____

_____

_____

_____

_____

_____

_____

_____

_____

_____

_____

Carolyn Monden

Carolyn Monden

_____

_____

_____

_____

_____

_____

_____

_____

_____

_____

_____

_____

_____

_____

_____

_____

_____

"

A good portion
of our fears begin in
childhood and when
we go to the source,
we start to understand
where the fear
started.

"

Step 4:

Put Yourself First

AFFIRMATION:
I pour into my cup.

These days we are expected to be all things to everyone at the same time. You know the drill, there's pressure to be a rock star at work, be in training for the triathlon, be president of the Parent Teachers Association and be the best significant other that chefs up gourmet meals and plans exotic trips. I'm exhausted just thinking about it, and sadly, we've all played this game of life with no chance of winning.

Breaking free from family obligations and societal norms feels wrong because we aren't taught to follow our internal cues. Instead, we're trained to blindly obey other's opinions on how we should behave, think and act, even if it goes against our core beliefs. No one teaches us to listen to our body and the gentle whispers of our soul when it says, "Hey, sit your butt down." We are so consumed with what's going on around us and maintaining control (even if we don't have control) that we fail to honor ourselves. How can you truly love something you've taken for granted? How can we expect others to listen to us when we won't listen to ourselves?

Two years after my detox, I suffered one of the biggest losses in my life. My aunt, my mother's sister, who cared for me and loved my brothers like we were her own, died from a massive stroke. My aunt Jackie was the glue that kept our family together. She organized all of the holiday get-togethers and birthday parties. She remembered everyone's birthday and meal preferences and bought special gifts. Best of all, she was available to me. *Always.* She was my rock, the person I wanted holding my hand for every major life event and she was there for everything. She was my North Star. The world was less ugly to me because aunt Jackie was in it.

My aunt had nineteen nieces and nephews, but she never had any kids of her own. She poured her love into all of us. And not just us, I used to joke that she never met a stranger. Aunt Jackie gave everyone she met her undivided attention and the blouse off her back if you needed it. No act of kindness was too large or too small.

Jackie died at 47, which is way too young. If I knew better I wouldn't have asked for so much from her. I would've insisted that we just swap stories instead of her making my favorite dish for my birthday. I would've fought for her to do more for herself. I would've told her to take it easy and relax. Aunt Jackie had conditioned us to lean on her, but she never asked (or demanded) that anyone hold her up.

My aunt's death taught me that nothing works without me. As an adult, I asked myself: Who is my family without me? What's the purpose of running myself into the ground if I won't be around to see my children grow up? What's the point of being Superwoman if I can't enjoy the life I've created with my husband?

When we don't prioritize our well-being and needs, we fight to have others do it for us. We scream at the kids, push our loved ones away, pull away from work projects, vent to girlfriends and argue with neighbors. We're an emotional mess because we don't know how to show up for ourselves. When we take care of ourselves, everything around us is at ease. I worry about myself for the sake of my family, which is not a selfish act. My children have a better, more attentive parent because I check in with the woman in the mirror. When I honor my feelings, I'm honest, kind to others, understanding and more forgiving.

This is because I hold space for myself. I don't wait for anyone to rescue me or recognize that I need a break. I don't fight to be heard, because I hear myself. I don't yell to be seen, because I see myself. I don't ask for love, because I love myself. None of this is easy. It took a while for me to take credit for how I show up in the world. It's my responsibility to validate myself. And you know what? I can and I do.

The idea of worrying about yourself is about taking ownership of how you want life to be, look and feel. How often have you used the phrase "If only..." or "I just wish..." or "Nobody understands..." Here's the truth: No one, but you, will understand what gives you peace and joy. Stop wishing for it. Wishes are for children. Grown women take responsibility for their lives. Do you want love? Love yourself first. Do you want attention? Attend to yourself first. Do you want to belong? Belong to yourself first. Everything that you've ever wanted has been waiting for you to find it within yourself, but your heart has to be open to it.

By putting yourself first, you discover who you are because what you desire becomes most important. Learning to be with self is how we begin to identify where we've said yes when we should've said no. We also examine why we said yes in the first place. When we commit to ourselves we create new standards for all of our relationships, instead of always compromising.

Now before I move on, I'm not suggesting that you neglect your family or use this chapter to behave in an unrighteous manner. No, this isn't a pass to be cruel. This is an opportunity to be true to yourself, to treat yourself with kindness because when you do, you have space to have compassion for others.

Here's a short list of what happens when you prioritize your needs:

- Less stress
- More rest
- Growing inner peace
- Clarity
- Direction and purpose
- More space to be there for others
- Greater understanding
- Less judgment
- Better health
- Better sleep
- Better sex
- Less doubt
- Improved relationships
- More self-esteem

Here's your affirmation for this part of your journey: I give myself permission to put me first.

Exercise 1: Make yourself happy

When was the last time you did something without seeking permission from a spouse, colleague or family member? Often, we're waiting for our turn, waiting for someone to realize that we need to be taken care of. It's common to wait for someone to reciprocate the deeds we automatically do for others. We wait for birthdays and holidays to be appreciated. There's no need to wait for a special occasion to make yourself happy. If no one has ever told you this, let me be the first to say it, you deserve joy.

Use this space to write down what makes you happy.

_____

_____

_____

_____

_____

_____

_____

_____

_____

_____

_____

_____

_____

_____

_____

What have you dreamed about doing, but didn't pursue because it isn't "normal" to the people around you?

_____

_____

_____

_____

_____

_____

_____

_____

_____

_____

_____

_____

_____

_____

_____

What do you like, or have always wanted to try, but aren't comfortable sharing with the people around you?

_____

_____

_____

_____

_____

_____

_____

_____

_____

_____

_____

_____

_____

_____

_____

Exercise 2: Get to know yourself

Sometimes, when we're working on our self-improvement, we get stuck running on a hamster wheel because we don't know what we really want. If you're a people pleaser, you were never encouraged to explore or have your own ideas. You live on autopilot and follow the people around you. But to seek happiness and find joy, you have to ask yourself, who am I? Believe it or not, the self-discovery process starts by looking at your childhood.

Here are some questions to help you get to know yourself:

What was your favorite thing as a child? Was it a game or activity? Stuffed animal? A place?

_____

_____

_____

_____

_____

_____

_____

_____

_____

_____

_____

_____

_____

_____

Carolyn Monden

What are your favorite memories growing up? (Hopefully, you have a sweet memory, no matter how rocky things were at home.)

_____

_____

_____

_____

_____

_____

_____

_____

_____

_____

_____

_____

_____

_____

What did you want to be when you were six years old? Who did you want to be when you grew up?

_____

_____

_____

_____

_____

_____

_____

_____

_____

_____

_____

_____

_____

_____

Remember this: We are born perfect with everything we need to survive. As adults, we spend time chasing the joy we felt as children, yet we've stopped trusting and believing in the magic in life. We conform to the conditioning of the world. Around seven or eight years old, we start to worry about what our classmates, parents or teachers think of us. And when they criticize us, our sense of wonder shrivels up like a raisin. (Or in my case, it made me question everything about myself. My whole existence was put into question because of my parents' choices.) However, this does not make you a victim. Tapping into your inner-child and healing from this place is how we discover our real selves. We collect insight from life experiences. It's a powerful thing when your inner child learns from those events and is able to use wisdom to find peace and understanding.

IT'S TIME TO JOURNAL.

This is how I feel about making myself a priority.

_____

_____

_____

_____

_____

_____

_____

_____

_____

_____

_____

_____

_____

_____

Carolyn Monden

Carolyn Monden

_____

_____

_____

_____

_____

_____

_____

_____

_____

_____

_____

_____

_____

_____

_____

_____

_____

_____

_____

"

When we
don't prioritize our
well-being and needs,
we fight to have others
do it for us.

"

Step 5:

Release Judgment

AFFIRMATION:
I accept myself.

I don't know about you but I come from a culture that uses passing judgment and talking smack (okay, gossiping) like it's a hobby. In the winter, my Dominican grandmother, mother and aunt would sit by the window of our New York City apartment in Washington Heights and talk about everyone that went by. No one escaped their harsh court of public opinion and nothing was off-limits. In the summer, they simply switched locations and took their sessions to the building's front stoop. My grandmother believed it was her duty to share the "news" with our neighbors.

I can't remember a time when I didn't feel judged by my family or neighbors. Shoot, I was judgmental too. Yes, five-year-old me was judging you. I know it may have seemed cute and funny but it wasn't. How we form opinions colors our perception and that influences our thoughts, which when based on judgment, can negatively affect our lives. This language of judgment is based on ignorance and lack of self-awareness.

On top of that, judgment causes division and it's a massive distraction. It's easier to sit in judgment of another person, than deal with our issues, right? It gives us the green light to avoid addressing our shortcomings and painful wounds. But here's the thing, releasing judgment is yet another layer of healing. Constant critical thoughts are unwanted noise.

Let me give you an example of how this plays out in day-to-day life. Maybe you know someone, let's call her Miss Attitude, and she wakes up one morning all judgy and critical because she didn't hit the gym the day before. Miss Attitude's self-condemning thoughts have set the tone for the day. Now her thoughts are followed by reasons why a run on the treadmill wasn't possible. The thought may subside, but it's now sitting off to the side like a juicy, red bruise.

This minor wound bothers Miss Attitude, but not enough to consume her (or so she thinks). This thought is followed by more reasons why she doesn't have time to exercise, including her workload and the long commute to and from work. There isn't enough time in the day to do everything and she can't stick to a schedule. These new thoughts take up space, which means she has little patience for others or herself, including the people on the crowded bus to the woman who asked her to hold the elevator. When she finally gets to work, she's irritated because everyone is getting on her nerves. Two-hours into Miss Attitude's day, a co-worker makes a comment about her project during a company meeting and she's ready to lose it. She feels attacked and she's doing her best to hold it in. Now, diving into work is now impossible. Miss Attitude goes over to another co-worker to vent, gossip and replay the encounter from the tone to the timing to the audacity of her comment. Miss Attitude's vibe toward her colleague can be quickly summed up to: Who does she think she is?

Question: Are you Miss Attitude? Are you always on the verge of flipping out? Do you swear your co-workers are talking about you behind your back? Do you jump headfirst into a rabbit hole of destructive thoughts? I'll be the first to admit that I was Miss Attitude, but I know that I'm not alone.

This scenario was my existence before I actively started to love and care for myself. I worried that someone would expose me for being a fraud. This behavior and thinking weren't just limited to work. This played out in every area of my life. My wrath was felt far and wide. I had no patience, which meant I had no friends. I judged others, but I judged myself the most. I'd get hired for a dream job and then doubted my ability. I'd make friends and get offended by harmless comments. I'd compare myself to them and cut them off whenever they triggered something in me. Too many people rubbed up against my invisible wounds and it would hurt.

In romantic relationships, I'd always have one foot out the door. I left at the first sign of trouble. My insecurity stemmed from my childhood and this feeling of not being wanted, so I beat everyone to the punch and I got rid of them before they could abandon me. I (mistakenly) believed it was my fate to never feel whole. This wasn't just a limiting belief, but it was the deepest, most painful wound.

My best defense was judgment. If I judged you, then I didn't have to face my pain. This path led me to more heartache, but after my daughter's birth, on some deep level, I knew I needed to get better if not for me than for her. I will be her example, the way my grandmother, mother and aunt Jackie were my influencers. I finally had enough. I had to do better. My judgment weighed heavy, but I couldn't keep carrying it around. How could I give my children my best, when I'd never experienced my best? How was I going to lead by example?

Here's your affirmation for this part of your journey: I am willing to release this judgment and forgive myself.

Exercise 1: List the self-judgment you use the most.

Releasing and healing require an awareness of the patterns that keep us stuck. By listing your judgment of self it is easier to notice when it comes up. For example, if you're at a swanky cocktail party and you get offended when someone asks where you went to school, you're concerned that person is judging your education. Even though I graduated from college, a question about education was a trigger. It sent me back to my days of attending underserved schools in New York City and leaving high school to take my GED. I'll dig into this in the next chapter.

_____

_____

_____

_____

_____

_____

_____

Exercise 2: Stop participating in judgment bonding.

Refrain from using judgment as a form of bonding. Some of your friends and colleagues may see it as conversation. But it isn't. You can't heal in this environment. If we are going to change our tone and release ourselves from judgment, we can't engage in this behavior. When in conversation with someone or in a group, gently suggest changing the topic. Speak about what's going well or something that's inspiring you at the moment. I'm not encouraging you to be fake, but refrain from passing judgment.

Exercise 3: I approve of myself.

When you have judgmental thoughts about yourself, like "I never do anything right. I'm not good enough or I always make things worse," stop and repeat this phrase instead. "I approve of myself." The bad habit of beating up on yourself didn't happen overnight nor will it disappear overnight, but you can force things to shift when you write a new script for yourself.

Exercise 4: Be mindful about being judgmental

So much of what we do mentally is set on autopilot. You may not even notice when judgmental thoughts pop up. Below, list your reoccurring thoughts about yourself. Seeing them on paper will help you to identify them and become more mindful. The goal is to stop using them altogether.

_____

_____

_____

_____

_____

_____

_____

_____

_____

_____

_____

_____

_____

IT'S TIME TO JOURNAL.

This is how I feel about
accepting myself—flaws and all.

_____

_____

_____

_____

_____

_____

_____

_____

_____

_____

_____

_____

_____

_____

_____

_____

_____

_____

_____

_____

_____

_____

_____

_____

_____

_____

_____

_____

_____

_____

_____

_____

Carolyn Monden

_____

_____

_____

_____

_____

_____

_____

_____

_____

_____

_____

_____

_____

_____

_____

_____

Carolyn Monden

"

Releasing
and healing
requires an
awareness of
the patterns
that keep
us stuck.

"

Step 6:

Practice Forgiveness

AFFIRMATION:
I am responsible for me.

Everyone has a story. We are shaped at the start of our lives by other people's choices. For some, it may seem unfair that so much of who we are is based on our parents' choices. My story (for better or worse) is intertwined with my mother's story. Her story is a product of my grandmother's choices and who my grandmother became is a reflection of her mother.

Forgiveness is a necessary part of loving yourself. Without forgiveness, we carry duffle bags and suitcases of wounds. Over time, this gets in the way of having a healthy relationship with yourself. If you're willing to forgive others, ultimately you'll be able to forgive yourself. Forgiveness is compassion in action. If we plan to write the outcome of stories that we've allowed to define us, we must forgive the mistakes that happened in the beginning and the middle. If I'm tasked with finding compassion for myself, then I have to find compassion for stories and the people that came before me.

This is where we practice compassion. How we feel about ourselves is how the world is reflected back to us. If you believe the world is out to get you, that is how you will respond to all circumstances. Sometimes, this is because you haven't released past actions and choices. Start here: forgive the mistakes, see yourself as a work in progress, understand that you're not the same person you were back then. You shouldn't beat yourself up (or beat up others) to survive. Take the armor off.

For many years, I carried the guilt of being a so-so student. I used to be ashamed about earning a GED, instead of finishing high school. I blamed my family and lack of guidance for not being in a better position to give me a greater life. Later, when I worked in politics, I was an insufferable mess. I beat myself up all the time. I replayed hurtful thoughts like: "I'm not as educated as my peers. I don't have the skills to compete." My insecurities showed up at work.

I made a name for myself in local politics. I carved out a niche. I was going to be the best Latina fundraiser and organizer in the south. Period. I had worked my way up to get a seat at the table. What I lacked in education, I made up for in grit. I pushed myself hard to get ahead. Without much experience, I became the head of the Latino Democratic Caucus of Georgia. This came with some notable mentions in Barack Obama's 2012 campaign, and I managed to work for the highest-ranking member of the Georgia House Democratic Caucus.

I even landed a job with Rep. John Lewis as his campaign field organizer. Trust me when I tell you that this was a big deal! But that didn't matter because I let my lack of confidence get in the way. I'd compare, begrudge and fail because I couldn't give myself credit. I'd quit many jobs because people didn't "respect me." Sadly, I did this for a decade because I couldn't forgive myself for my fear of failure.

What I didn't know wasn't the real problem. People were willing to see past gaps in my learning. My attitude led to my downfall. If I'd learned to have compassion and grace for what I didn't know and didn't have, I would've learned more and I would've become comfortable in my skin. In the end, I left politics because it wasn't a good fit for where my life was headed. It was a challenging career, however, it wasn't part of my new vision. Had I been less hard on myself, I would've learned this lesson much sooner.

When I left politics, I still blamed others, including my former boss and my co-workers for my need to hit the escape button. I wasn't ready to take responsibility for my actions and behavior. Eventually, I got sick and tired of my own crap. I walked away from my destructive narrative and I'm proud to report that I forgave myself for staying too long where I didn't belong. I forgave myself for being messy and making a mess back then. Compassion allowed me to take ownership of my mistakes. When I left politics, I gave myself time to figure it out. I committed to healing and learning about myself without the pressure to please others. I was a little easier on myself in the new phase of my life. This phase granted me permission to see past my compulsive reactions of blame and shame and change my bad habits for the better.

Most people don't realize that forgiveness is for you, not the other person. Forgiveness allows us to begin the healing process. We can't move forward if we're holding on to past stories, histories and behaviors with all of our might. Understand this: refusing to forgive someone is baggage, which only gets heavier as you get older. (Don't be the bag lady Erykah Badu sang about.) You must let it go and forgive. In the self-love journey, this is an important part of the process.

I became the woman I am today because I forgave the girl that brought me here. I'm grateful for everyone who participated in my lessons because it allowed me to heal. I can't blame anyone anymore. It took some time, but I finally learned that I possess the water and sunlight that I need to grow.

Here's your affirmation for this part of your journey: I give myself the gift of forgiveness and I release my past.

Exercise No 1: I'm willing to release the script that keeps me stuck.

Write down the script that keeps you trapped in a state of unworthiness. These stories (your script) are the thoughts that show up every time you feel scared, ashamed or unloved. This limiting belief keeps us going in circles, but writing it down helps identify and change the script and forgive ourselves for this false narrative.

Sample script: "Nothing good ever happens to me. I don't have luck when it comes to relationships, money or love. I'm never going to have the life that I want. I'm not smart enough or pretty enough to achieve my dreams."

_____

_____

_____

_____

_____

_____

_____

Exercise No. 2: I take responsibility for how I feel and how I want to feel.

For this exercise, write about how you *feel* on a good day. Focus on how you feel, not what you're doing. We think the activity matters, but it's how we feel that makes the moment special. This puts the responsibility back on your feelings. By doing this, you learn to wield your personal power, which no one can take away from you.

_____

_____

_____

_____

_____

_____

_____

_____

_____

_____

_____

_____

AFFIRMATIONS FOR FORGIVENESS:

- I am not my past.
- I forgive others as I learn to forgive myself.
- I am not my mistake.
- I am responsible for how I feel.
- I chose to forgive.
- God loves and forgives me.
- Everyone is doing the best that he or she can.
- I free myself from pain.
- I forgive those that have hurt me.
- I am not my pain.
- I release all negative beliefs.
- I am worthy of compassion and kindness.

IT'S TIME TO JOURNAL.

This is how I feel about giving
myself a well-deserved apology.

_____

_____

_____

_____

_____

_____

_____

_____

_____

_____

_____

_____

_____

Carolyn Monden

Carolyn Monden

_____

_____

_____

_____

_____

_____

_____

_____

_____

_____

_____

_____

_____

_____

_____

_____

_____

"

If you're
willing to forgive
others, ultimately
you'll be able to
forgive yourself.
Forgiveness is
compassion
in action.

"

Step 7:

Practice Acceptance

AFFIRMATION:
I commit to me.

Life can be dark and gloomy when we experience heartache, pain and grief. But it can be beautiful, loving and joyful too. Life is a journey of all of these emotional experiences. Merriam-Webster's dictionary defines it this way: "An act of travel or passage from one place to another," such as the journey from youth to maturity or a trip through time.

As we move from youth to maturity, we must strive to stay present and build resiliency. That's the purpose of our lives. Moving through heartache to joy and then back without significant harm to ourselves is the practice of acceptance. Sometimes, we think hard times are experiences that should happen to other people. We've all said this aloud: "Why me?"

During difficult times the tendency is to shy away from our feelings or avoid them and just keep busy, but being frantic only adds to the storm.

An example I use with my clients is to be like a tree. Some trees in Georgia grow to be 80- to 100-feet tall. This doesn't happen overnight, which means the tree has endured many storms. It may wave back and forth during tornadoes and severe thunderstorms, yet the tree is unmoved. In the fall, the tree releases what she no longer needs. Bare and alone, she prepares herself to hold snow and ice. She may bend, but she doesn't break and through it all, she stands strong. You never hear about the tree fighting nature or unfair conditions. The tree does not fight the storm because she knows this is a part of what she'll face during her time on earth. In the last five years, I made it my mission to be more like the 80-foot white pine trees in my front yard.

A good acceptance practice is to be in the moment. Feelings are indicators that we need to pause, feel and go within. There in the pause is where lessons are learned. This is the act of showing up, being still and holding space amid a storm. This is the love we're so desperate to have. In these moments, when no one can make the situation better, all we can do is accept ourselves. I had to do this when I worked in politics. It took years for me to realize that my actions contributed to how I handled work tasks and connected with colleagues.

The lesson here is this: You are not your pain. You are not your emotions. You are not your experience. You are the woman *behind* the experience. The most significant accomplishment in my journey was learning to be still with myself and practicing self-acceptance. But healing and loving myself wasn't an overnight achievement. Acceptance isn't a one and done situation, it is a practice. The practice of loving yourself is a commitment. You have to commit to this every morning and every moment thereafter. The journey of one passage to another requires remembering that we are on a purposeful path and we're being blessed with the tools to survive life's storms.

The following are some key things you should practice.

Practice being okay with uncertainty. I hope you understand that we don't control what happens. We can only control how we react. For instance, I had no idea my aunt Jackie would die when she did. She wasn't sick. There was nothing anyone could do about it. I could have let the experience become another hole in my heart. Instead, I asked myself: "What can you learn from this?" There was no way to prepare for that sudden loss. But aunt Jackie's death taught me that every day is important, because it could be my last day with my family. Now, I know that whatever may come, I'm only here to witness it, to experience it and that's all. I affirm: Life is precious and treasures may be hidden in the unknown. I don't want to miss a moment of it.

Practice letting go of controlling outcomes. This one is hard but it's achievable. For every upset or setback, I affirm: Things are always working out for me.

Practice sitting with your fears. I imagine the worst-case scenario. And then I remind myself through positive affirmations, that my fears are just thoughts. This gives me the strength to change my perception of things. I affirm: If I change the way I look at things, the things I look at will change. (This beautiful quote is borrowed from self-help author and motivational speaker Dr. Wayne Dyer.)

Practice being honest, even at your worst. The start of my mental and emotional struggles was connected to me having my way. In that mindset, we are bound to be challenged. I'm not desperate to be right. Being wrong and realizing that you're wrong can be a blessing (at times). This acknowledgment opens you up to acceptance. There is much to learn in life. I affirm: I am not here to be perfect. I am here to learn new things.

Practice following your heart and soul. Trusting myself is a big part of self-love and healing. Knowing the difference between my thoughts (the conditioned voice in my head) and the gentle whisper of my soul is vital. Again, we struggle because we need the pull to match the thoughts and that will never be. I give myself space to know that my thoughts, in an attempt to protect me from harm, will find danger in everything, while my heart and soul know best. When I am uncomfortable, I allow my soul to guide me and not the story in my head. I affirm: I am not my fears. I trust my heart.

Practice holding space for yourself when you need love. We suffer when we believe we aren't getting what we deserve. I've made it a practice to myself whatever I need and this allows me to love myself and others without conditions. This practice also opens me up to creating healthy boundaries. Knowing how to hold a loving space is all anybody wants. To hold space means to give yourself the time and compassion needed when you are unsure and are in need of love. To give someone space is to love them without judgment so they are able to pick themselves up and start again. It is unconditional love. If I can give it to myself, I can recognize when someone offers me love without conditions. To receive love, I have to love myself first. I affirm: I cannot ask for something I am not willing to give to myself.

Practice being vulnerable (which I have done by writing this book). I didn't know that I could do this. At first, I worried that no one would read it, but I've published it to empower women. And I know this message will reach those hungry to feel good about themselves. Good or bad this is me. Real. Vulnerable. Imperfect. Authentic. Acceptance, as a rule, opens the door for change with little damage. When we resist and fight what is right in front of us, that's when we cause a chain reaction. Damage is caused when we blame and mistrust others. This causes us to ruin relationships and the ones who are closest to us pay the price for our lack of vulnerability. When we are unwilling to accept and share our feelings, we look for other reasons why things aren't going as planned. It's up to you to see and accept your wound, your fear, your power and most of all, your purpose.

Practice surrendering to a new version of yourself with ease. The more at ease I am with it all, the more I can be my authentic self, the more I grow in my womanhood. Being vulnerable is how I face my fears and work my way through them. Being vulnerable is my superpower as a mother, wife, sister, friend, coach, co-worker, etc. I am an example of love. I affirm: My life is an example that I am doing the best I can. It doesn't matter how many times I get it wrong.

Practice doing hard things (in the words of Glennon Doyle). Life is messy and complicated in every sense of the word. It is seldom black or white. There is every single shade of grey. The grey areas require me to look at what is right in front of me and this may mean that I have to do or deal with things I'm not prepared to handle at the moment. But I don't resist, my soul knows what it needs to do. It is only hard if I am not healed and I cannot see what is right in front of me with love in my heart. What needs to be done is always present and waiting for me to take the leap and do it. I affirm:

Life isn't out to get me. Life is an experience. It's a once in a lifetime vacation and I must practice making the most of it.

Here are a few more things I practice saying to myself. Now it's your turn to say some of these aloud.

- It's okay to be wrong.
- It's okay to choose me first.
- It's okay to say no.
- It's okay not to know.
- It's okay to change your mind.
- It's okay to want to love.
- It's okay to want acceptance.
- It's okay to create the love and acceptance that you want.

Here's your affirmation for this part of your journey: I love myself.

Loving yourself is the foundation of a fulfilled life. It's a gift we give to ourselves. Very little scares me these days because I've faced my darkest demons and given myself grace. I've stopped building from a place of lack and filled in the holes with unconditional love. In the past, I wouldn't have expected anyone to give me this much unconditional love and acceptance. Slowly, I found the real me and she is dope, empowered and kind. She is loving, smart and strong. She worked hard to get here and works hard to stay here.

Exercise No 1: Make a commitment to create the life you've always envisioned. Be open and accepting. Understand that this isn't the end, rather this is only the beginning.

For this exercise, dream big to create a new vision for your life. Let it be gigantic and outrageous. What have you always wanted to do? If money and time were not a factor, what would you do? What's the vision? Oprah Winfrey said, "Your life isn't about a big break. It's about taking one significant life-transforming step at a time." Think about that. What step can you write down on paper that will propel you in the direction of your wildest dream? I'll go first. Writing this book is one of my transforming steps. I honored a promise that I made to myself. Now it's your turn. Today, promise to love yourself and commit to constantly improving your life one transforming step at a time.

Below, write down how you will commit to yourself. Be specific.

_____

_____

_____

_____

_____

_____

IT'S TIME TO JOURNAL.

This is how I feel about making room for self-love.

_____

_____

_____

_____

_____

_____

_____

_____

_____

_____

_____

_____

_____

_____

Carolyn Monden

_____

_____

_____

_____

_____

_____

_____

_____

_____

_____

_____

_____

_____

_____

Carolyn Monden

_____

_____

_____

_____

_____

_____

_____

_____

_____

_____

_____

_____

_____

_____

_____

_____

Carolyn Monden

"

Acceptance
isn't a one and done
situation, it is a
practice. The practice
of loving yourself is a
commitment.

"

Conclusion:

Be Like The Sunflower

"Be a light onto yourself."
—*Buddha*

Writing a book, or creating anything by yourself, can be a lonely process. I had to motivate myself when doubt crept in to poke holes in my confidence. Creating a mock cover for *Love Yourself First* was the ultimate confidence boost. It also served as a reminder about the promise I made to myself.

As I made my way from first to final draft, I hired a professional designer to create this cover. I sent the artist my favorite colors, pictures of me and the book's premise. She designed multiple covers, but this one, filled with sunflowers, immediately touched my heart. It felt like the perfect representation of self-love and led me to research this special flower. I had no idea about the sunflower's spiritual meaning.

Carolyn Monden

The more I read about how the sunflower symbolizes "faith and adoration," I knew this was the perfect image for *Love Yourself First.*

Sunflowers also signify happiness, confidence and loyalty. Any botanist will tell you that the sunflower has strong roots and turns herself to the east to soak up the sun's light and follows the sun's westward movement. But when the sun sets, the sunflower turns to face the east, again, to prepare for the next day's journey. In the right conditions, a sunflower can grow 16-feet tall.

Sunflowers, in my opinion, are the epitome of self-actualization. She is self-aware of her love of the sun and in her self-acceptance, doesn't mind facing this powerful energy source to receive what she needs. The sunflower is self-respecting in her choice to stand in her power and grow as fast and tall as she needs to be her full self. A sunflower knows her time on earth is limited, so she is who she is without apology. That is self-love. The sunflower knows herself. She does not concern herself with how much taller she gets in comparison to other flowers in the field. She seeks to be her best, most authentic, individual self. The sunflower receives the sun's warmth and recognizes how she must show up in the world.

The sunflower also brings joy to the world by being herself and she naturally attracts the right connection. Unlike humans, she doesn't wait for someone to provide nourishment, instead she loves herself first. Give yourself permission to be like the sunflower and only receive the best for yourself. Hold your head up high as you take up space. Learn to love yourself and let that adoration grow deep and strong. Bask in the light and find yourself whole right where you are. Like the sunflower, be true to yourself, and only give to others once you are full. Protect everything and everyone that is good for you. Live with full commitment to the light and wisdom within. Accept your place and be there without concern. You are allowed to exist. You deserve to be here. You deserve to be happy. Like the sunflower, you have a purpose. Love will show you the way.

Acknowledgments

To my husband, Chad, thank you for pushing me to honor my commitment to myself. More importantly, thank you for seeing my potential when I didn't or couldn't see it. You never gave up on me or us. I love you.

Benjamin and Charlotte thank you for allowing me to be your mother and for sharing me as I pursued this dream to write a book, especially during the pandemic. I promise when you look back on those days when I was tied to the computer, it will all make sense.

Thank you to Taiia Smart Young, my writing coach and editor. This book wouldn't have been possible without you. Your encouragement and the confirmation that these stories need to be told is beyond what I could've asked for in the author-editor relationship. Thank you for gently pulling the writer out of me. Here's to many more books together.

To my friends and clients, you are the reason for this book. I am honored to have you in my life and cross paths with you. I'll be forever grateful for our shared journey. Thank you.

About The Author

Carolyn Monden is an intuitive life coach. She specializes in removing stumbling blocks to help clients uncover their true desires. Carolyn is passionate about empowering others to develop a deep connection to self. She believes self-awareness is a key element to finding and loving yourself and it's her purpose to teach, interpret and guide the conversation as clients find their life's purpose. Before becoming an intuitive life coach, she spent 20 years in community building, business and marketing. Carolyn, her husband and their two children live in the East Cobb suburb of Atlanta.

Thank you for reading

Love Yourself First:

7 Steps to Finding & Healing The Real You

If you enjoyed this book, please leave an online review.

Let's connect on Instagram: @mondenwrites

To book an appointment for Soul Coaching, visit www. carolynmonden.com.

As your Soul Coach, I will work with you to navigate your life, uncover your desires and remove limiting beliefs and roadblocks. Our sessions will be empowering, uplifting and truthful.